Kindred Beginnings

Your journey. Our support.

Coloring Your Way Mindfully Through Your Family-Building Journey

By

Chrissy Beswick & Lynn Polin

Graphics by

Mike Goldstein

Kindred Beginnings

ISBN: 978-1-7356420-0-0

Every journey is valid.

I never personally struggled with fertility.
As a big sister to my adopted siblings,
I witnessed first hand how my parents
fought to build their family, their way.
As a best friend, I stood by my friend as
she built her family through her fertility journey.

I saw it all. The joy, the tears, the bravery, and
the outright fear. I was there for shots, test results,
scans and surgeries. What came from all of this was
a deeper understanding of how fertility affects so many,
in many different ways. Although I will never fully understand this journey,
I validate the courage and determination of each person along the path.

Put on your oxygen mask first. They say that on a plane because it's true. This journey is hard. Real and raw. But you can make it through. Give, and get grace. Allow yourself to feel the things and to move on. Taking care of ourselves is vital to being there for those we love, for having a stronger mind-body relationship, and for making room for joy in our lives.

With love,
C

Dear Fellow Warrior,

I see you. I hear you. I empathize.

I have a BIG story too:
6 years.
10 IVF cycles.
5 retrievals with over 60 eggs retrieved.
24 embryos.
12 PGS genetically tested.
4 fresh transfers.
7 frozen transfers.
2 miracle girls.

The journey twists and turns as you navigate your way to what it is you want-a baby. Your struggle is real and is part of honoring your story. But balance is needed too.
Self-care.
Self-compassion.
Self-love.
This is where we need to focus our energy because you, Fellow Warrior, have done nothing wrong. It is so important to take care of ourselves because when we are stressed our hormones become imbalanced, we are more prone to sickness, our relationships suffer (including with yourself) and we have less energy. Managing stress through daily self care that becomes a healthy habit is key to living a happier and healthier life for you, your partner, and your future child(ren).

Be kind to yourself. Embrace your beginner's mind by connecting your mind, body and spirit as you color your way through the stress of family-building, giving yourself permission to be embraced by grace and loving-kindness.

Always
Bring
Your Own
Sunshine!

I AM CAPABLE OF
AMAZING THINGS

I FOCUS ON
THE POWER OF
NOW

I'm doing
the best
that I can

I AM
HAPPY

I AM
KIND
TO
MYSELF
I AM
KIND
TO
MYSELF

MY
BODY
IS
WORKING
PERFECTLY

I AM
STRONG!

I am worthy of
love

I release all negative thoughts

I will be an
amazing mother

I will conceive at
the perfect time.

my
baby is
coming
to me.

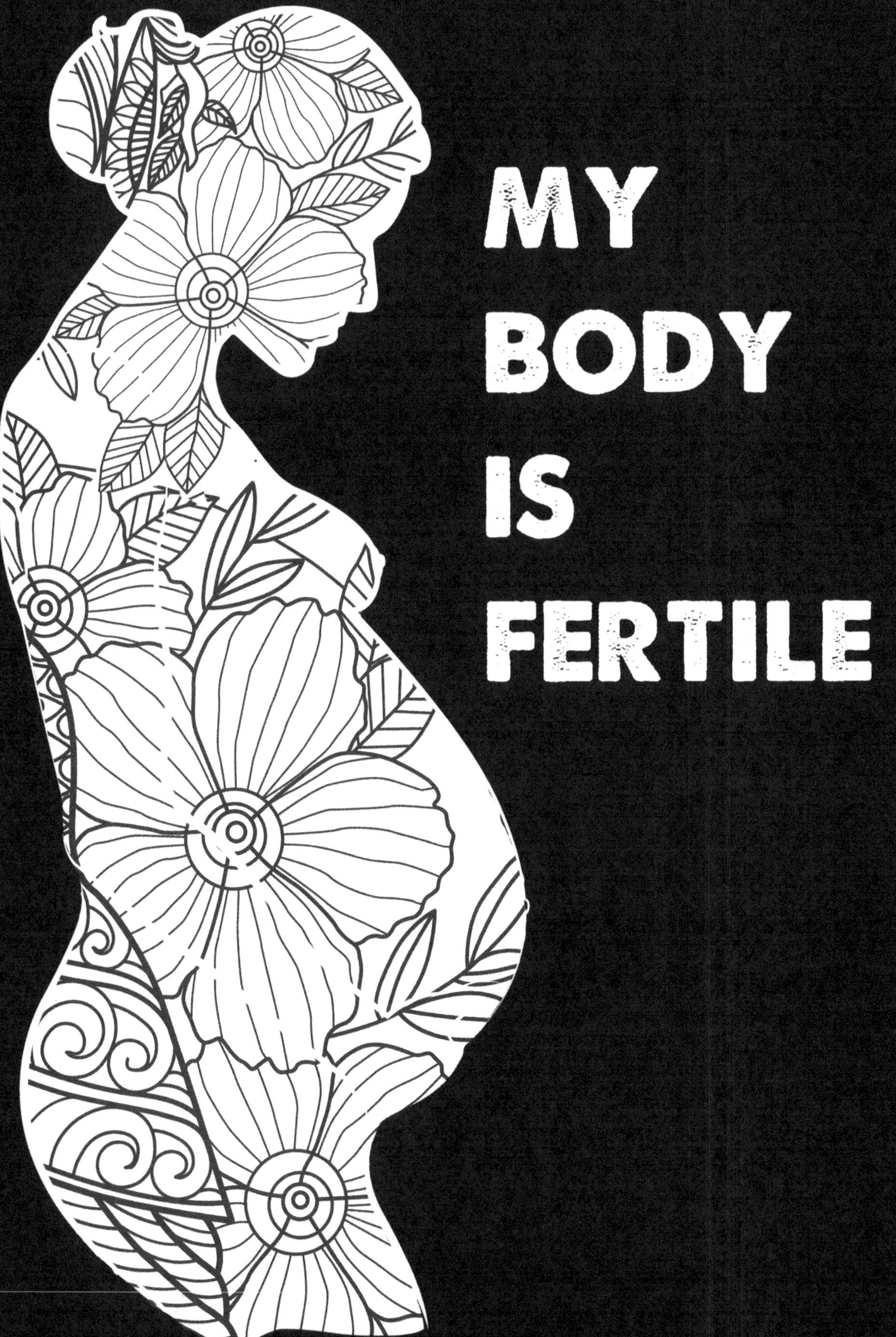

MY
BODY
IS
FERTILE

I surround myself
with people who
lift me up.

I Matter

The struggle is part of the story.

Doing my BEST

I'M READY TO BE A MOM.

HELP
SPERM
GET TO
EGG!

www.ingramcontent.com/pod-product-compliance
Lightning Source LLC
LaVergne TN
LVHW061226100826
845148LV00004B/880

9781735642000